SHARE
THE ROAD

Café

Rugby, North Dakota
Geographical Center
of
North America

Published by Ed Morris Photography™

Book design by AkinsParker Creative. www.AkinsParker.com

Printed in the United States of America

ISBN: 978-0-615-27817-9

WWW.MAYORSACROSSAMERICA.COM

_____

www.EdMorrisPhotography.com

MAYORS ACROSS AMERICA

······················· **FORWARD** ·······················

As my father tells it, my older brother Newth and I were somewhat over served when we came up with the idea of riding our bicycles across the country. That may be true, I don't remember. We were both moving to California. Newth was moving to Newport Beach to begin his career in engineering, and I was moving to Santa Barbara to attend the Brooks Institute of Photography. To us, it made perfect sense.

It took us a little more than two weeks to gather our gear, plan the route, and convince our parents we were serious. I suspect that as we departed on this 3,600-mile bicycle ride, the last thing either of them expected was a phone call just 38 days later, saying, "we made it, we're in Seattle".

My brother and I are both strong willed individuals. When we set out, our goal was the same; to ride bicycles across the United States. However, in the first few days on the road we came to realize that we had different agendas. Newth was intent on doing the ride as fast as possible. I was intent on taking photographs. The two are mutually exclusive of each other, and he ultimately won. I harbor no resentment. I am in fact grateful and indebted to my brother for pushing us both to achieve at the highest level. I am proud of what we accomplished as a team. Riding just shy of 100 miles per day for 38 days, without support, is an impressive feat by any measure. Still, I could not help but feel that we had missed something. The contrast between the rural communities and larger metropolitan areas was striking. The hospitality and good nature of virtually everyone we met was mind opening. The vastness and diversity of landscape and culture was profound. I knew there was a story there that I had missed.

As I began planning this second trip, I struggled with how to tell that story photographically. I knew, that even at a slower pace, time would be a major constraint. Since this project was to be completed for course credit through Brooks, I was able to consult with my advisor, Ralph Clevenger. He patiently demanded that I find a focus in the story before he would sign off on the project. As I sat in his office for one of our last meetings I relayed a story from the first trip.

"Our original route maps have these little notes on each town about what services they offer. For one of the towns in which we stopped there was a note saying the town would make available the park pavilion with restrooms and showers. All you had to do was go to the Mayor's house, the address was provided, and ask the Mayor for the key... The Mayor!"

··

{ FIFTY-NINE DAYS }

An eight-week, 3,600 mile bicycle journey
documenting the American Mayor.

{ Introduction }

···

My friend and riding partner, Tim Hovey, and I have been asked many times why we chose to ride bicycles. The simple answer is that walking would take too long. Bicycles provide the perfect pace. Over the 10 week period that we were on the road we averaged around 60 miles per day.

We carried all of our gear with us. Fully loaded with tents, sleeping bags, power bars, film, cameras and all of the other necessities, our bikes weighed a torturesome 90 pounds. Over the course of the trip we rode through three mountain ranges: The Cascades, The Rockies, and The Appalachians. It usually surprises most to learn that the Appalachians are by far the most brutal for cycling. In the tall and steep mountains of the West the only way to allow traffic through is to cut passes, so you essentially ride up one side and down the other at a controlled grade. Granted, going up is a hard won 3-4 mph, but the back side is an exhilarating coast, at speeds upwards of 55 mph. In the older rolling Appalachians they simply pave over what might be called 'hills' of fifteen percent grade or more. The moment you crest one, your heart sinks as you see them repeating off into the horizon.

···

The wind can be either your friend or your enemy, never both at once, decidedly one or the other. At your back it will hurry you along your merry way, blowing kisses and well wishes on your journey. At your side it will ridicule you, like a tormenting sibling running, grabbing your handlebars and nudging you in the gut. At your front it will challenge your very sanity, laughing, nose to nose in your face, as you struggle to gain ground.

Most nights we camped. Many towns offer up their parks and pools for cyclists passing through; we humbly and excitedly accepted this hospitality. A swim in a pool or a hot shower were rare luxuries. On several occasions we had folks invite us to stay in their home, which we gratefully accepted. About once a week we were treated to a hotel room.

Occasionally this was at our own expense, though quite often a local TV or radio station covering the project would pick up the tab. In one instance, when a severe storm warning threatened to make camping hazardous, a local citizen insisted on paying for a hotel for the night. Our long days of riding and tracking down and meeting with Mayors occasionally left us setting up camp in the dark just off to the side of the road.

Food is fuel in an absolute sense when you are engaged in something like riding a bicycle across the country. Breakfast is America's meal and there is no doubt about that. There was not a town we passed through, that had a restaurant, that lacked a good breakfast. We often ate breakfast twice a morning. When you're riding a bicycle everyday, all day, you can eat bacon, waffles, eggs, butter, pretty much anything, with reckless abandon.

My intention from the beginning was to document small towns of America and demonstrate the contrast between those towns and larger cities. The Mayors, being elected officials, proved to be the perfect vehicle for illustrating the general hospitality, character, and economic status of a town or city, given our relatively limited time.

The pace and freedom of riding a bicycle is ideal for absorbing a small town, a countryside, or a thriving city. This helped me to create a more informed interpretation of each town. If we spent an entire day riding through nothing but corn, soy, or wheat fields, it was a safe assumption that the upcoming town would be very agricultural. In the case of St. Paul, MN, where it took us three hours to get across "town", it was obvious that it was a large and thriving city.

Except where it was necessitated by the size of the city, our encounter with each Mayor was not arranged ahead of time. My intention was to capture a candid

portrayal of each Mayor. We would literally roll into town and inquire as to the Mayors whereabouts. Local citizens, public libraries, and post offices were very helpful in finding the Mayor. There were many towns and cities where, for various reasons, we could not locate the Mayor. Only twice did we make contact with the Mayor and were refused a visit, once in Chicago and once in a town of about 300.

In all but one case, the Mayor chose the location for the photograph. It is important to note that a large percentage of the Mayors we met with were not full time, at least in terms of compensation. In such cases, where the Mayor held a job outside of city hall, the job often dictated the location. Conversely, the minute to minute schedule of full time Mayors of large cities usually dictated a precise time and place. In all cases, the location of the photograph was critical and informative.

This series of 87 portraits is presented here, in its entirety, for the very first time.

{ THE ROUTE }

The Northern Tier route, established by the Adventure Cycling Association, attracts numerous adventurers each year. During our trip we met a number of fellow cross-country cyclists. The route begins in Anacortes, Washington. It heads east over the Cascade Mountains and across Idaho. Very near the Canadian border, it continues east into the vast state of Montana, over the Rocky Mountains, crossing the continental divide at Glacier National Park, and into North Dakota. At Rugby, North Dakota (the geographical center of North America) the route heads southeast, crosses Minnesota, and then turns south along the Mississippi River occasionally crossing into Wisconsin. At Davenport, Iowa, the route turns east, heading across Illinois, Indiana and into Ohio. At Canton, Ohio, we departed from the established route and headed southeast just across the southeastern most corner of Pennsylvania, a very short time in West Virginia, and on into Cumberland, Maryland. At Cumberland, we picked up the Chesapeake & Ohio Canal towpath, which winds along the bank of the Potomac River and culminates in the heart of Washington, District of Columbia. From there it was a relatively short ride into my hometown, Severna Park, Maryland and then just 15 miles into Annapolis by way of the Baltimore & Annapolis Trail.

{ **MAYOR JERRY DAVIS** }

KETTLE FALLS, WA

POPULATION: 1,527

· ·

"I was on the Council for 8 years before
I became Mayor. It's not anything you're
going to retire on; it's community service."

{ MAYOR ROBERT ANDERSON }

COLVILLE, WA

POPULATION: 4,988

....

"City Hall is where it all happens."

{ **MAYOR DEE OPP** }

NEWPORT, WA

POPULATION: 1,921

....

"You need to listen to the citizens. You can't
always do what they want you to, but you give it
a try and see if it works out. The citizens are the city."

{ **MAYOR TOM HARTLIEP** }

PRIEST RIVER, ID

POPULATION: 1,754

"I'm afraid I can't spare much time. I am the Mayor, but I
also own this garage, and I'm the preacher at the church."

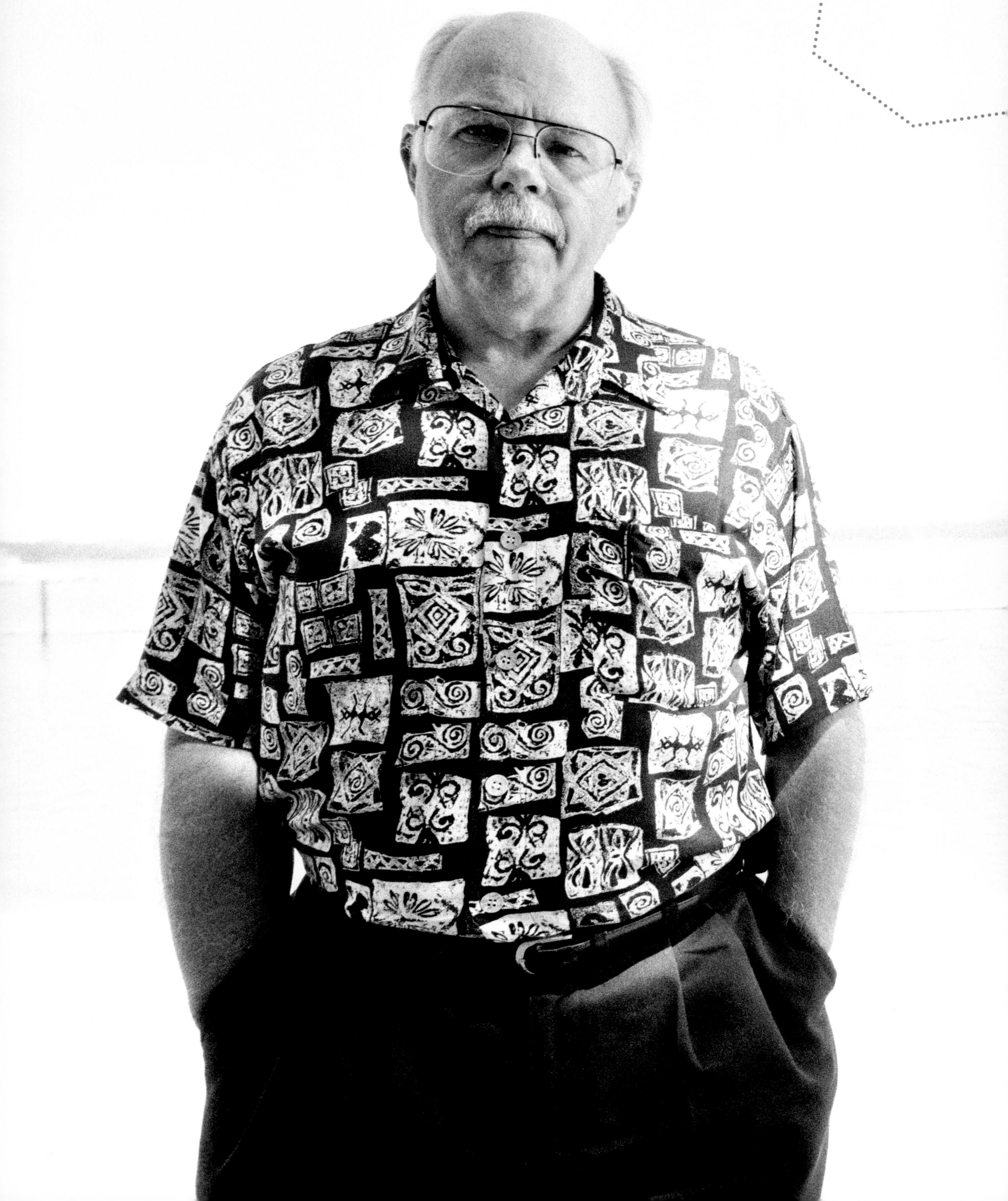

{ **MAYOR PAUL GRAVES** }

SANDPOINT, ID

POPULATION: 6,835

....

"Most Mayors are not prepared to handle everything

that goes on in the city, a good staff is critical."

{ MEETING MAYORS }

··

In the photographic community we say 'shoot' not 'photograph'. It is critical, however, that when you walk into a City Hall, you don't say something like, "We're here to shoot the Mayor".

All of our encounters with Mayors, with a few exceptions, were extremely brief. This was due, in no small part, to our need to make our miles each and every day regardless of terrain and conditions. It also had to do with the Mayors' schedules. In most cases, regardless of the size of the town or city, Mayors are busy people. In large cities the job of Mayor demands a minute-to-minute schedule. While the scale of the job may be different in smaller communities, the scope is the same and the pay is quite often nominal. Unless retired, those Mayors must keep a full time job as well. In either case, the Mayors' time is precious, and we had to be respectful of that. Although our meetings were usually brief, they were always meaningful.

··

{ MAYOR MARGARET MJELDE }

KOOTENAI, ID
POPULATION: 441

···

"No... they're not my children.

I run a small day care from home."

{ **MAYOR LINDA REED** }

CLARK FORK, ID

POPULATION: 530

....

"I'm really too busy. If you want, you can meet

me at the bridge on the way out of town."

{ **MAYOR GARY HALL** }

COLUMBIA FALLS, MT

POPULATION: 3,645

. . . .

With very little exception, the position of Mayor
is a full time one. Only in a relative few of the
largest cities does the position pay a full time salary.
Most Mayors have some sort of additional employment.

{ CHAIRMAN EARL OLD PERSON }

BLACKFEET NATION, MT

POPULATION: 10,100

....

"I am not a Mayor.

I am the Tribal Chairman of the Blackfeet Nation."

{ MAYOR MARION CULLETON }

CUT BANK, MT

POPULATION: 3,105

· ·

"Working together makes good things happen.

As Mayor I enjoy working on reasonable solutions to

problems and seeing our community grow and prosper."

{ MAYOR WAYNE WARDELL }

CHESTER, MT

POPULATION: 871

．．．．．．．．．．．．．．．．．．．．．．．．．．．．．．．．．．．．

"I never did seek the office of Mayor.

I was appointed about twenty years ago and have been

re-elected ever since. The only way you get out of this

job is to die. I don't plan on doing that anytime soon."

{ **MAYOR PHYLLIS LEONARD** }

HAVRE, MT
POPULATION: 9,621

"People don't like change and they don't like having

the water bill raised to be able to make the changes.

The only satisfaction I get will be the fact that I can live

in this town and be sure I have water when I turn

the tap on and sewer when I flush the toilet."

{ **MAYOR BILL OEHMCKE** }

CHINOOK, MT
POPULATION: 1,386

"I don't have an agenda. When there's a problem
I don't have a slant. We just go after it and get it fixed."

{ **MAYOR DIANNE PETERSON** }

HARLEM, MT
POPULATION: 848

....

"I think it is always a different struggle

for towns bordering a reservation."

{ THE WEATHER }

If you are going to ride across the Northern United States, I recommend doing so in the summer. I've done it twice and, provided you don't mind a little 100+ degree heat, the weather is perfect. The heat was at times overbearing, in fact record breaking, but with plenty of sunscreen and water, we managed. Only a handful of days did we have to deal with rain of any significance. The evenings typically cooled off for comfortable sleeping. Our mission on this trip was to meet and photograph people, so summer was ideal. Kids are out of school. Public works projects are underway. People in general are out and about and accessible.

There is one element to the weather noticeably absent here. It is an element so notorious, so loved AND so hated by cyclists it deserves space all to itself.

{ CHAIRMAN JOE McCONNELL }

FORT BELKNAP RESERVATION, MT

POPULATION: 2,959

Not a Mayor, Chairman Joe McConnell, is Tribal Chairman

and President of the Community Council. The reservation

is home to the Assiniboine and Gross Ventre tribes.

{ MAYOR BYRON EREAUX }

Malta, MT
POPULATION: 2,120

. . . .

"Our industries are not prospering.

It is a daily challenge to provide jobs

and economic development."

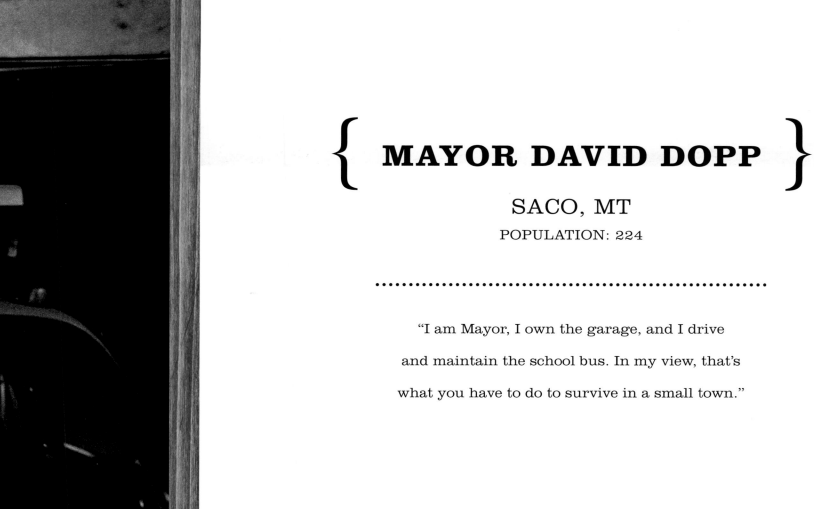

{ **MAYOR DAVID DOPP** }

SACO, MT

POPULATION: 224

"I am Mayor, I own the garage, and I drive
and maintain the school bus. In my view, that's
what you have to do to survive in a small town."

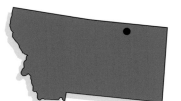

{ **MAYOR WILMER ZELLER** }

GLASGOW, MT

POPULATION: 3,253

· ·

"As Mayor, I have worked to get our
infrastructure to be the best for a community
our size. I also work for the school district
as janitor. I'm quite proud of our community."

{ **MAYOR DALLAS O'CONNOR** }

POPLAR, MT

POPULATION: 911

"The Mayor should be elected to protect the City's
assets. So we must act to do just that, regardless
of personal relationships. When you plow the roads
you start in the city and work out from there."

week 4, day 24

{ MAYOR GORDON OELKERS }

CULBERTSON, MT

POPULATION: 716

· ·

"I was born and raised here.

My direct family has lived in Culbertson since 1910."

{ CITY COMMISSIONER JAMES YOCKIM }

WILLISTON, ND

POPULATION: 12,512

· ·

"The Mayor is out of town, but we would

like our city to be represented in your project."

{ MAYOR CLARE AUBOL }

NEW TOWN, ND
POPULATION: 1,367

....

"In a community like ours, where you have issues of
jurisdiction, you have to be aware of everyone's needs. Our city
is technically inside the Fort Berthold Reservation. Our most
important project has been to develop our water resource to
ensure people in the rural and tribal areas have water."

{ 89 }

{ MAYOR CARROLL ERICKSON }

MINOT, ND
POPULATION: 36,567

Minot is nicknamed the "Magic City" because

of its growth during the early 20th century.

It was settled in large part by Scandinavians.

{ **MAYOR CHUCK SCHMIDT** }

Surrey, ND
POPULATION: 917

"We heard about you guys on the radio, so I thought
I'd ride my bike to meet you. This is the same school
I went to as a kid and graduated from."

{ THE FOLKS }

....

Even at the relatively slow pace a bicycle allows, it is possible to get so focused on the riding itself that you miss the important part: interacting with the good folks who populate the towns and cities across the vast, diverse and beautiful landscape. Two factors really forced us to engage and interact with locals in every community through which we passed: eating virtually all of our meals in local restaurants and seeking out the Mayor.

More often than not, locals were as curious about us as we were about them. Although the dynamics were certainly different depending on the size of a given town or city, in the overwhelming majority of situations, we found the folks to be kind, helpful, and hospitable. Folks would pay for our meal, sometimes anonymously, invite us to stay in their home, camp in their park, swim in their pool and in one extraordinary act, pay for a hotel room and slip us a one hundred dollar bill.

....

MICKEY IBARRA
ASSISTANT TO THE PRESIDENT AND
DIRECTOR OF INTERGOVERNMENTAL AFFAIRS

(202) 456-7060
FAX (202) 456-6220

THE WHITE HOUSE

{ MAYOR HILMAN ULLAND }

GRANVILLE, ND

POPULATION: 107

....

"The largest long term task of my office

is maintaining adequate finances."

{ **MAYOR STEVE FOSTER** }

TOWNER, ND
POPULATION: 574

· ·

Mayor Foster works as a quality control

manager at the Winger Cheese factory.

{ **MAYOR DAVE CICHOS** }

RUGBY, ND

POPULATION: 2,939

· ·

"Our industries such as Rugby Manufacturing

and the hospital are prospering, but I believe

it is important to bring new business to town."

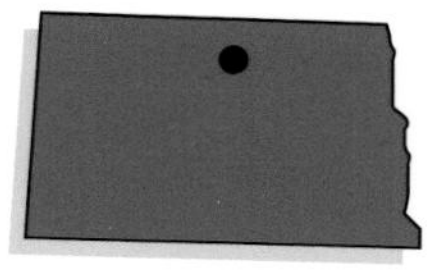

{ **MAYOR SEBASTIAN HAMAN** }

ESMOND, ND

POPULATION: 159

. . . .

"I'm retired. If something needs

to be taken care of, I can do it."

week 5, day 29

{ MAYOR MARK SEILER }

NEW ROCKFORD, ND
POPULATION: 1,463

Mayor Seiler and his brother manage the Bison Grill.

{ MAYOR ALLAN METZGER }

CARRINGTON, ND

POPULATION: 2,268

· ·

"In rural America it's about moving forward each

and every day, otherwise we'll be moving backwards."

{ MAYOR BOB BOULVITSCH }

GLENFIELD, ND
POPULATION: 134

....

"I don't mind participating, but it will have to be here. I've got to get this lawn finished… I believe people elected me because the town has a number of projects to get finished before winter and they feel I can get them done."

• • • •

"One of the toughest daily challenges we face is the out-migration of young people. Seventy percent of our population are elderly people."

{ **MAYOR ROBERT BAKER** }

COOPERSTOWN, ND

POPULATION: 1,053

Cooperstown is primarily an agricultural community.
They are fortunate to also have several industries, a school
and a hospital. Mayor Baker, at age 84, works energetically to bring
new business to town and to maintain services and infrastructure
with the interest of preserving and improving the community.

{ **MAYOR GARY IHRY** }

HOPE, ND

POPULATION: 303

"The most important characteristics of a Mayor are

Leading by doing and investing in your town.

We are working to build our infrastructure so that

Hope should be in good shape for 30-50 years."

{ FUEL }

Staying hydrated is absolutely one of the most important things. Riding in the summer makes it even more essential. We had several days in a row of 108-degree weather. The heat was, at times, overwhelming. The 'chip tar' rural roads became sticky. The black asphalt became a radiator. We drank a continuous flow of water and sweated so profusely that we took surprisingly few pit stops. We were drinking gallons of water per day.

We didn't cook. That decision was made before we left, with a couple of considerations in mind. Most obvious of these is that cooking takes time, utensils and food. We knew at the outset that between the riding and finding and photographing Mayors, our time would be pretty well committed. Additionally, the stoves, utensils, and food would have added considerable weight to our already overburdened bicycles. More important however, was having the experience of walking into the diners and restaurants and getting the odd looks. Sitting down and having conversations with the local folks, telling them about the project and seeing if they might know where to find the Mayor was an informative and entertaining part of our trip. On more than one occasion we were the source of great amusement at our seemingly endless consumption of food. The photography aside, we probably spent more money on food than anything else.

WYOMING
The Christmas City

Home 319-488-3169
505 W. Green
Wyoming, Iowa

Rick Watters

141 West Main Street
Wyoming, Iowa 52362
Phone 319-488-3970
Fax 319-488-3976

PANHANDLER PIES
RESTAURANT & BAKERY

REX WILLIAMS, OWNER

BREAKFAST • LUNCH • DINNER
120 S. 1st ST.

SANDPOINT, ID 83864

(208)263-2912

CATTLE CAPITAL OF NORTH DAKOTA
TOWNER
PROSPEROUS FUTURE
NEWMAN

{ **MAYOR BRUCE FURNESS** }

FARGO, ND

POPULATION: 90,559

"Maintaining public safety is the number one issue,

but adequate water supply is a long term priority."

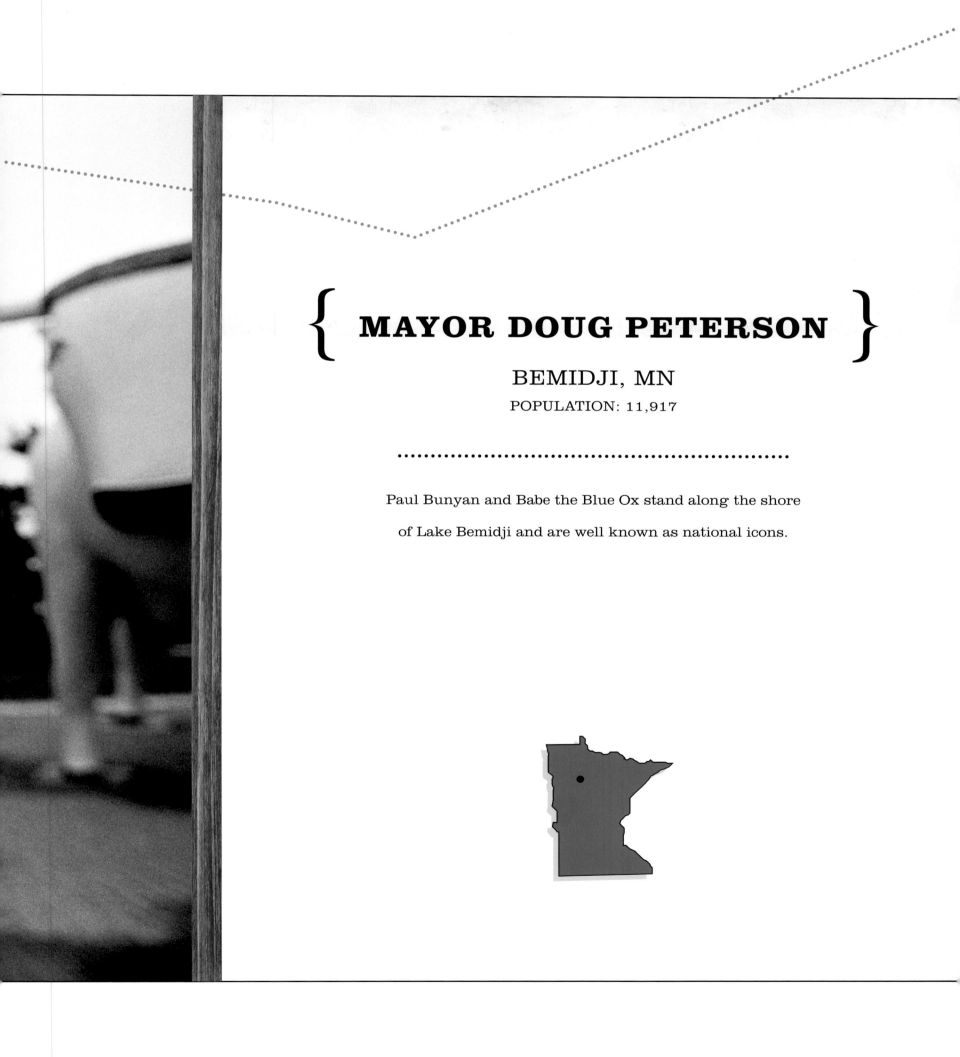

{ MAYOR DOUG PETERSON }

BEMIDJI, MN
POPULATION: 11,917

Paul Bunyan and Babe the Blue Ox stand along the shore

of Lake Bemidji and are well known as national icons.

{ **MAYOR BOB LUNDEN** }

DEER RIVER, MN

POPULATION: 903

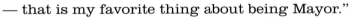

"I am the Chief of Police as well as Mayor. Both are full time jobs; the rewards are few. Seeing that the employees and citizens are happy with the city, jobs, and each other — that is my favorite thing about being Mayor."

{ **MAYOR JUAN LAZO** }

GRAND RAPIDS, MN
POPULATION: 7,764

....

"The Yellow Brick Road is a tribute

to Judy Garland. She was born here and

we have a Judy Garland festival every June."

{ MAYOR KELLY McCAULEY }

WARBA, MN

POPULATION: 183

....

"When I was a kid we never had recreation.

My goal has been creating a Rec. Department

and building a hockey rink, baseball diamond,

playground and others."

{ MAYOR PENNY OLSON }

McGREGOR, MN
POPULATION: 404

. . . .

"The hardest thing for me has been turning down

calls for help from communities outside of town.

It's a compliment because it means we are collectively

a community, but legally I am bound to serve this town."

{ **MAYOR GLORIA WESTLING** }

McGRATH, MN

POPULATION: 65

....

"One of the local girls got in a bit of trouble.
She is a gifted artist, we felt that having her
paint the stones to look like buildings in town
was a punishment that fit."

{ **MAYOR MARY SCHWARTZ** }

MORA, MN

POPULATION: 3,193

....

"Mora is a sister city to Mora, Sweden. We do a lot of

activities together. They have the largest Dala Horse.

This is the largest in the U.S."

{ **MAYOR MARLYS PALMER** }

CAMBRIDGE, MN

POPULATION: 5,520

....

"Our largest long term task is the

reconstruction of downtown."

week 6, day 37

{ DEPUTY MAYOR CLELL BONE }

ISANTI, MN
POPULATION: 2,324

....

In the Mayor's absence, the Deputy Mayor

represents the community.

{ SHUT-EYE }

···

When you spend the better part of every day riding a bicycle, the only thing you crave more than food is sleep. It is never hard to fall asleep after a long day of riding. Most of the time we camped. Camping is convenient; when you're finished riding for the day you can pull off the road, put up your tent and go to bed. When you are exhausted, it can be hard to make the extra effort in scouting out a good spot for setting up camp. I personally have an incredible knack for pitching my tent on a slope. However it is always worthwhile, when camping in public parks, to look around for in-ground sprinklers. Nighttime is the only time when, within the realm of decency, certain parts of the body can be allowed to breathe. Thus, in the event of a pre-dawn dousing, you will invariably be sent scrambling across the park, bicycle and tent in tow, wearing... well...nothing at all. I have also learned, the hard way, that sprinkler systems are often set sequentially.

Camping is truly a wonderful way to completely experience a place. It is not, however, without it's inconveniences. Rain, of which we had very little, can make camping very uncomfortable. A sleeping pad is far from a portable mattress. And if the mosquitoes don't carry you away, they will do their best to devour you whole. We enjoyed our occasional hotel stays. It was always a welcomed reprieve; a hot shower, soft bed, laundry (in the sink), and even a little television.

···

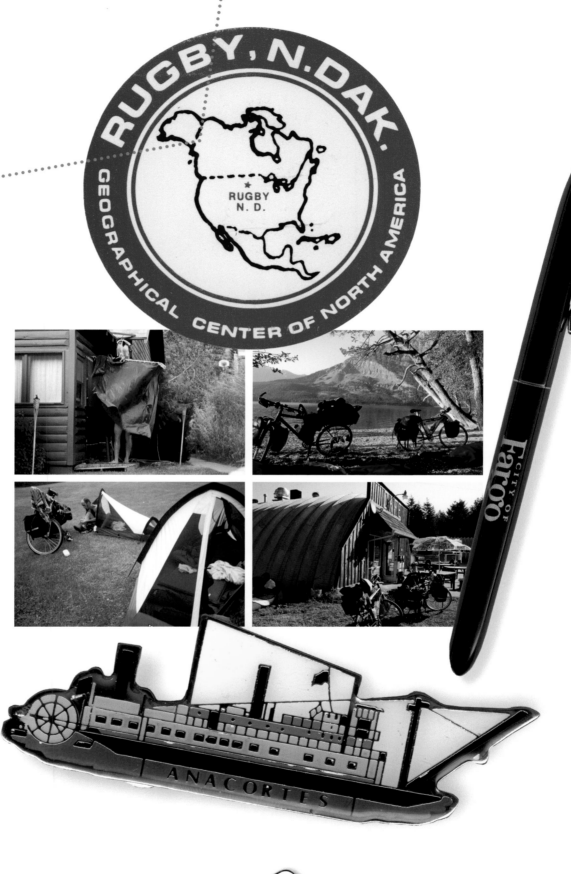

{ **MAYOR NORM COLEMAN** }

ST. PAUL, MN
POPULATION: 287,151

· ·

"I've discovered, in my conversations with many mayors of small towns and larger cities, that the job is really the same. The scale is different but the job is the same. My greatest frustration has been the cynicism people have about the government and politicians. Large cities; small cities — in every one the Mayor is putting in a lot of time and energy to serve the community."

{ MAYOR JAY KIMBLE }

STILLWATER, MN
POPULATION: 15,143

. . . .

"The bridge is an icon for our town. That's why I had
it painted on my Harley. We need a new bridge for the
increasing traffic; getting that going is the biggest task
of my office. We will keep the old bridge so pedestrians
and cyclists can enjoy the beauty of St. Croix River."

{ MAYOR CARL BROMMERICH }

FOUNTAIN CITY, WI

POPULATION: 983

....

"A good Mayor is honest, willing to listen

and willing to work hard with and for the people."

{ MAYOR JERRY MILLER }

WINONA, MN
POPULATION: 27,069

··

"The statue is Princess Winona, our namesake.

The hills she is looking off to will be protected,

but our town remains challenged with maintaining

the beauty and nature of Winona, while still allowing

for some growth and development."

{ **MAYOR MIKE POELLINGER** }

LA CRESCENT, MN
POPULATION: 4,923

....

"In the early 1850's John S. Harris moved here from back East.

He was recognized nationally for growing fruit in colder climates.

Because of his grafting and numerous attempts to produce

a hearty tree we wound up with over 140 varieties of apples.

Our history has largely to do with fruit and farming."

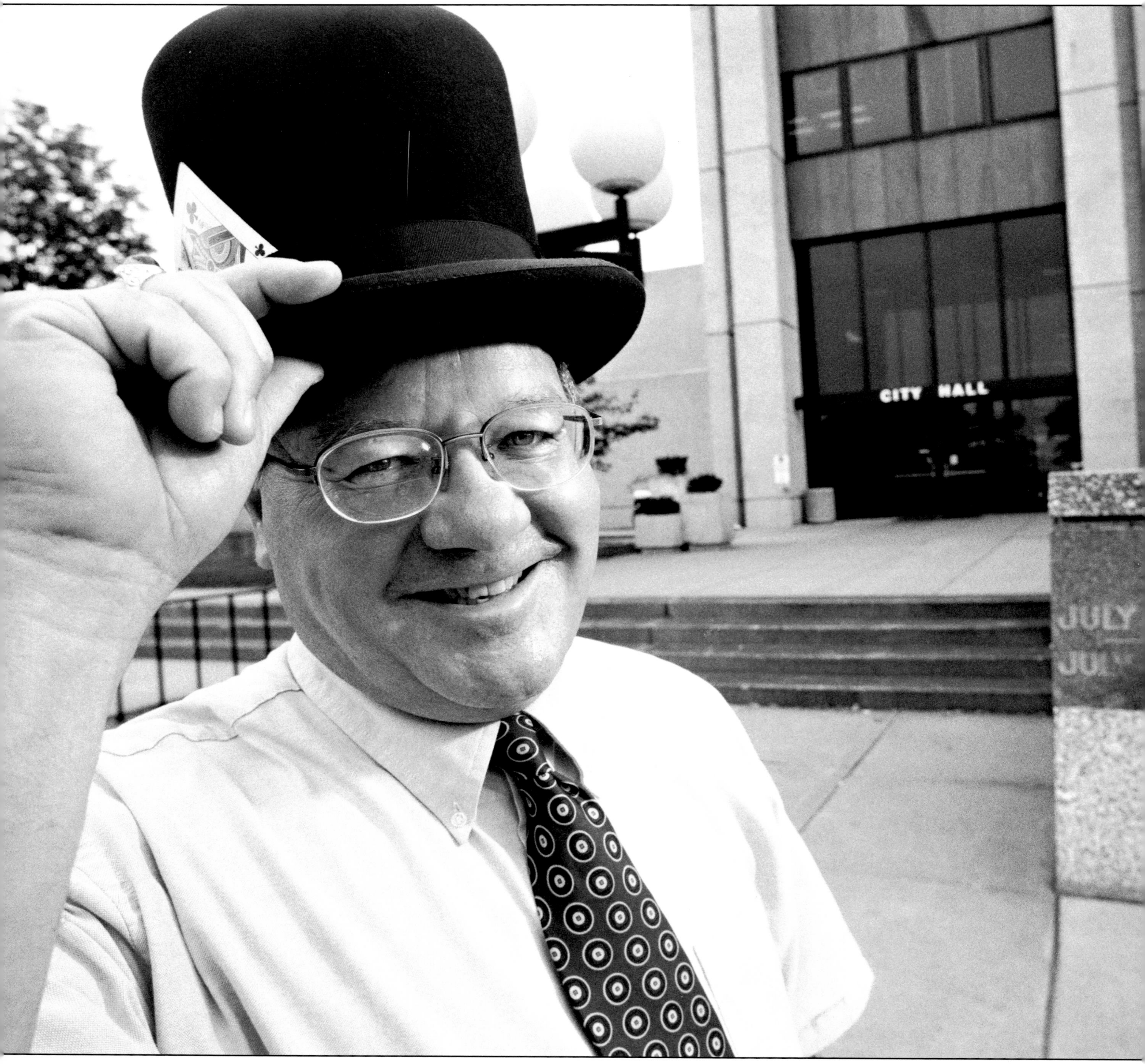
CITY HALL
JULY

{ **MAYOR JOHN MEDINGER** }

LA CROSSE, WI

POPULATION: 19,718

··

"It's an old river tradition for the

Mayor to greet and welcome visitors."

{ **MAYOR BOB BULMAN** }

NEW ALBIN, IA

POPULATION: 527

....

"I was a fireman for 35 years. Now I'm Mayor,

a part time farmer and a full time grandpa."

{ MAYOR VERNON BLIETZ }

LANSING, IA

POPULATION: 1,012

··

"The largest tasks of my office are improving
streets, bridges, and community pride."

{ MAYOR ELEANOR SOULLI }

MARQUETTE, IA

POPULATION: 421

....

"The railroad has been instrumental

throughout the history of Marquette."

week 7, day 43

{ MAYOR GERALD BLOCK }

Guttenberg, IA
POPULATION: 1,987

••

"We were having some difficulties here in the city with

the Police Department. We had some unethical management

which caused terrible turnover and issues with the citizens.

Having been a police officer for 23 years, I was a good

person to get that reversed."

{ MAYOR RON BOECKENSTEDT }

NEW VIENNA, IA
POPULATION: 400

....

"One of our students came up with the slogan.

Everyone in town liked it. So we went with it."

{ GOING POSTAL }

General Delivery is a rather old-fashioned service the post office continues to offer. A package can be addressed to General Delivery and the package will wait at the specified post office until the recipient happens to arrive. This served us well, as we could have film and supplies sent ahead of us. We also frequently mailed packages back with keepsakes, unneeded gear and shot film. To the credit of the United States Post Office, not a single package was lost or damaged. A trip to the Post Office was also the most efficient way to find the Mayor.

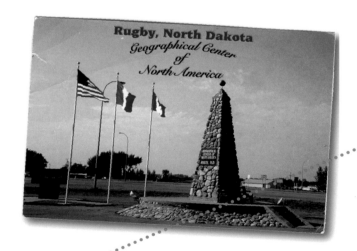

DEER RIVER CITY

Date Incorporated
January 22, 1898

City of Deer River
208 SE 2nd Street
P. O. Box 70
Deer River, MN 56636

DEER RIVER, MN
-PM 17 2001
56636

34

Mr. Ed Morris, Photographer
P.O. Box 40601
Santa Barbara, CA 93140

93140X0601

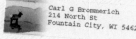

Carl G Brommerich
214 North St
Fountain City, WI 54629

LA CROSSE, WI 546
PM
13 NOV
2001

34

ED MORRIS PHOTOGRAPHER
P.O. BOX 40601
SANTA BARBARA, CA.
93140

93140+0601

{ **MAYOR ALAN GIBBS** }

DYERSVILLE, IA

POPULATION: 4,035

"We are a wealthy 'ag' town with a strong tax base, so there really aren't too many struggles with being Mayor. We also have the Basilica, 1 of 35 in the country. We've got the 'Field of Dreams' where the movie was filmed and RC Toys; they make miniature farm replicas, and have a toy show twice a year. A larger part of our economy is tourism."

{ MAYOR RICH KNEPPER }

CASCADE, IA

POPULATION: 1,958

....

"Be involved in your community; it is the citizens that make

the community. Everything is a reflection of the citizens."

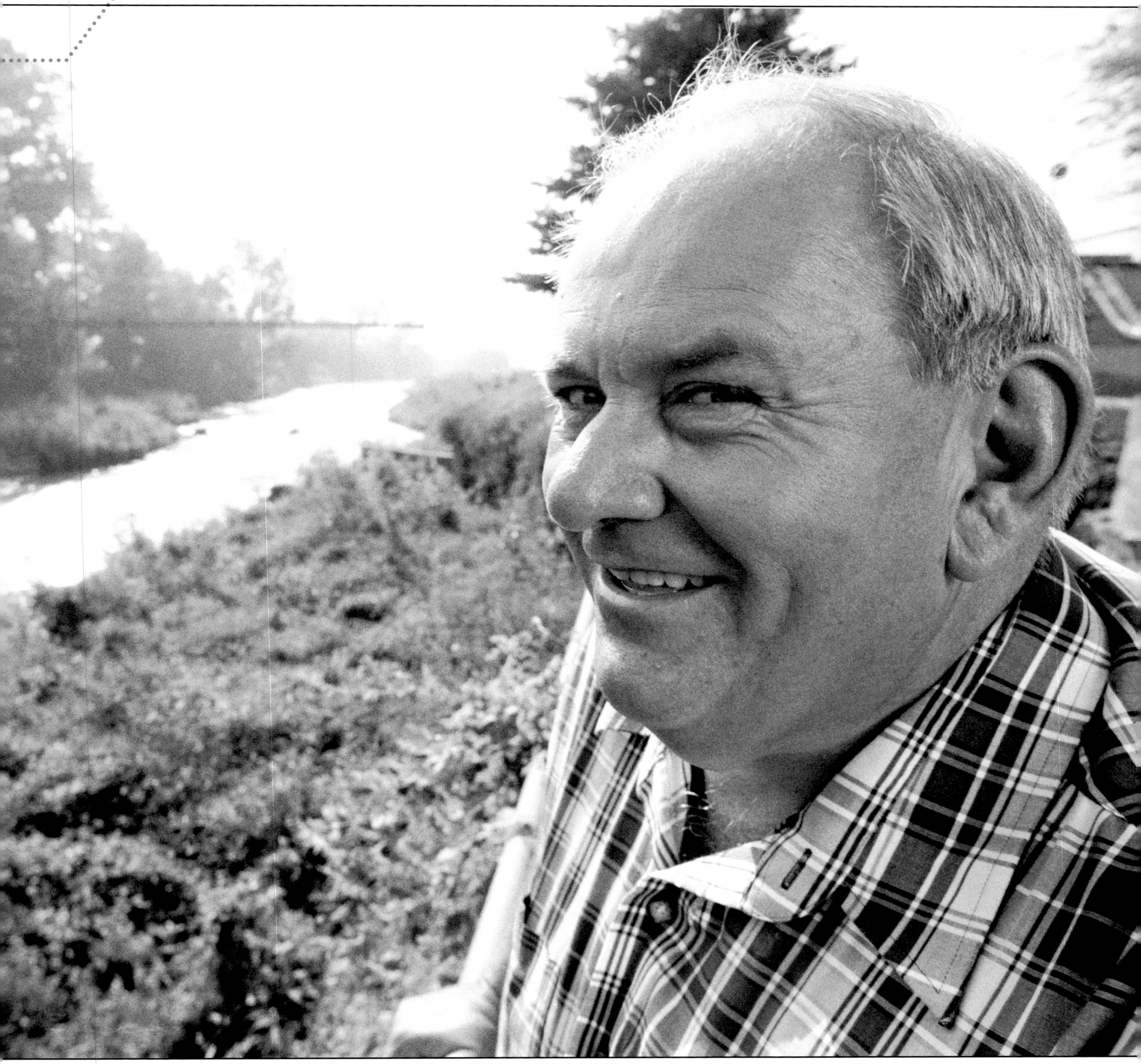

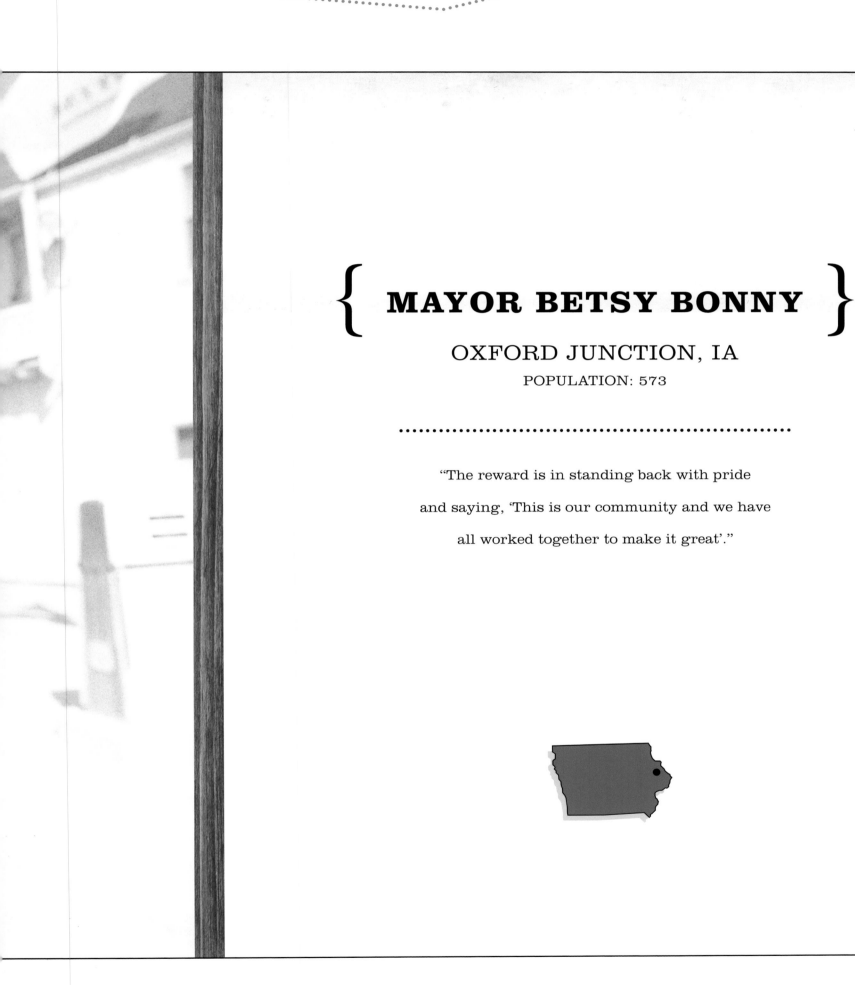

{ **MAYOR BETSY BONNY** }

OXFORD JUNCTION, IA

POPULATION: 573

"The reward is in standing back with pride
and saying, 'This is our community and we have
all worked together to make it great'."

{ **MAYOR DAVID WENDT** }

BENNETT, IA

POPULATION: 395

. . . .

"Knowing how to apply for the grants is the largest
part of the job. The government pretty much tells
you how it's gonna go. In the community you have
to work with the elderly as well as younger, newer families
to reconstruct the older homes."

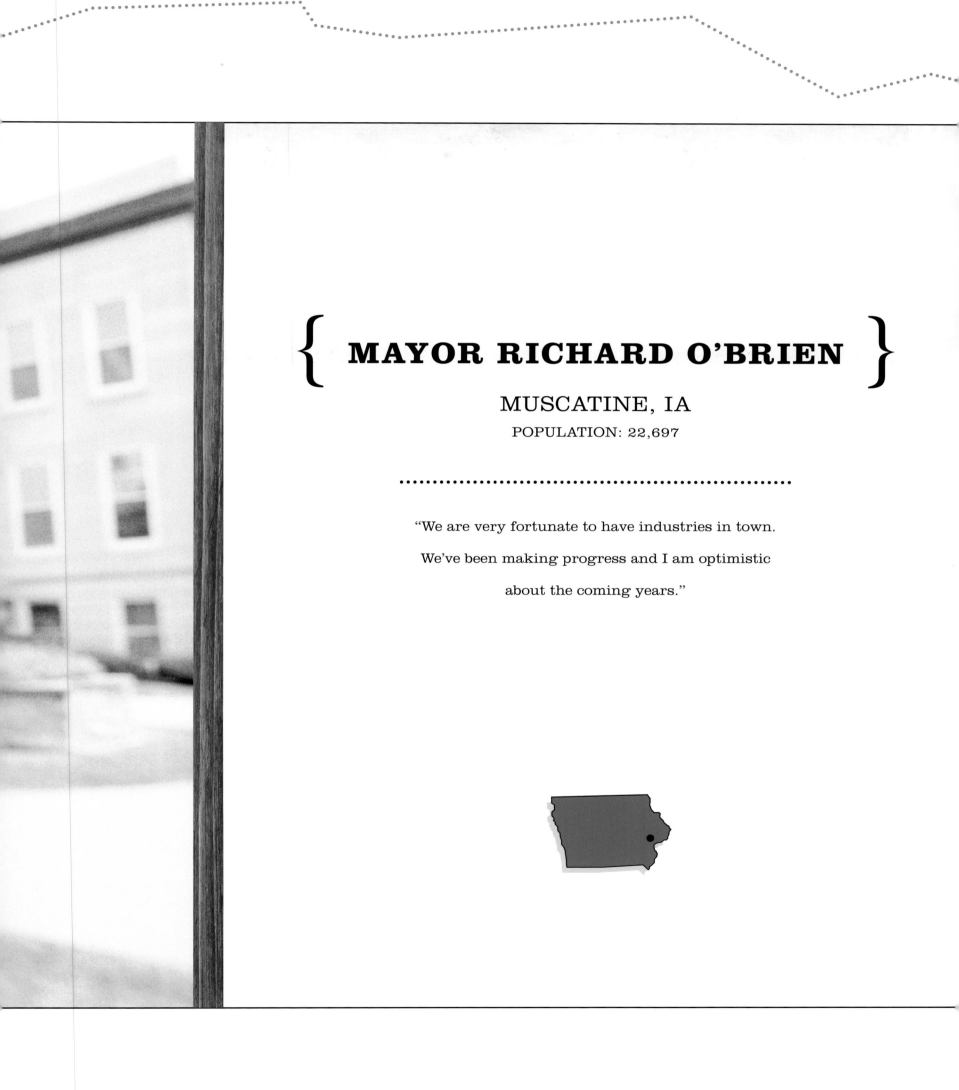

{ MAYOR RICHARD O'BRIEN }

MUSCATINE, IA
POPULATION: 22,697

....

"We are very fortunate to have industries in town.
We've been making progress and I am optimistic
about the coming years."

{ **MAYOR WILLIAM LARKINS** }

ORION, IL
POPULATION: 1,713

....

"I think everyone should have a crack at public office,

small or large, especially if you live in a smaller town."

{ **MAYOR JOLENE ALLEN** }

CAMBRIDGE, IL

POPULATION: 2,180

· ·

"It's a real advantage for a small rural town

to be the county seat."

{ **MAYOR JIM BURNS** }

KEWANEE, IL
POPULATION: 12,944

....

"I'm golfing early in the morning.

If you can meet me before that I can do it.

Otherwise, I'm afraid I'll have to pass."

{ SADDLE SORE }

Comfort on a bicycle is all about ergonomics. It is not about cushioning. The most important thing is to have your sit bones in the right spot on a good saddle. Your handgrips are another very important factor. I never quite got mine right. My left thumb, index and middle fingers were numb from about day 3 right on through the end of the trip. It's something with which I just learned to live. You can not pad your way out of discomfort. There is a certain level of discomfort to which you become accustomed, and it does not ever really go away. If it did, I would still be riding. Many people have asked if I had heavily padded riding shorts. Well-padded shorts do exist, but it is the chamois cloth, which "wicks" away moisture, that makes them an important asset. In terms of comfort over the long haul, this is probably the most important piece of equipment. Ideally, you start each day with a dry, if not clean, pair of shorts...ideally.

{ **MAYOR JAMES KUPEC** }

WENONA, IL
POPULATION: 1,065

....

"You said to take you somewhere that 'says' Wenona."

{ **MAYOR STEVEN WHITMAN** }

CULLOM, IL

POPULATION: 563

....

"The Mayor had to be appointed by the board.

We were all sitting in a meeting and it came to a point

where I stood up and said, 'Well I guess I'm it,' and I was."

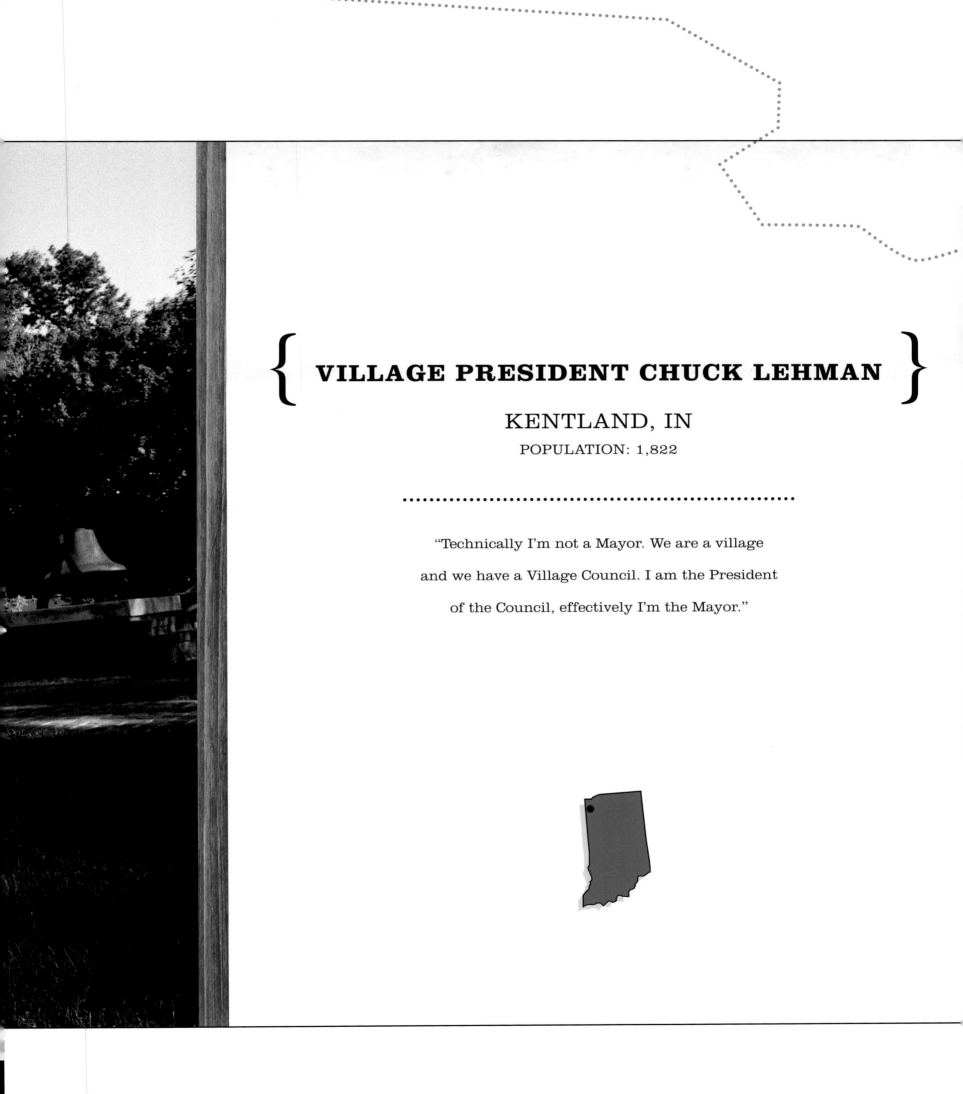

{ VILLAGE PRESIDENT CHUCK LEHMAN }

KENTLAND, IN
POPULATION: 1,822

....

"Technically I'm not a Mayor. We are a village

and we have a Village Council. I am the President

of the Council, effectively I'm the Mayor."

{ **MAYOR ROBERT FOX** }

MONTICELLO, IN

POPULATION: 5,723

....

"A local artist made these signs for everyone in the office."

{ MAYOR RICHARD HETTINGER }

LOGANSPORT, IN
POPULATION: 19,684

....

"I ran on two things. First, to improve our infrastructure;

I believe you need infrastructure for people to come to

your town. Second, to help the community get along; our

community is undergoing significant diversification and we

have recognized the need for all of us to learn to get along."

{ **MAYOR RICHARD BLAIR** }

PERU, IN

POPULATION: 12,944

· ·

"Myself and some others didn't like the way things
were going. We felt like we needed some new blood.
At the time that was me. Now we try to provide the
most services we can, for the least amount of money."

{ **MAYOR TERRY ABBETT** }

HUNTINGTON, IN

POPULATION: 17,450

....

"I'm extremely busy right now, but I'd like to show you

the court house; it's something I'm very proud of."

"When you are chief elected official, in this case of the second largest city in the state, you become an expected if not designated spokesman for the region. Boundary lines don't mean what they used to years ago. The mayor of a large city just out of necessity must have regional focus. We're affected by what they do and they are affected by what we do. The need to collaborate is critical for the success of small cities and small towns. If you can get people together to mutually agree on what the problems are and set aside our differences, that is the Mayor of the future."

{ THE WIND }

People often ask what aspect was the most challenging, or if there was anything in particular that made us want to quit. I think if you are determined, nothing is going to make you quit. However, on a trip of such magnitude, you are likely to evaluate your motivations from time to time. Riding mountain passes is actually not that bad. It can be grueling and it takes a lot of mental determination, focus, and sometimes even a lack of focus to grind up those passes. But there is a goal. You reach the summit and then it's usually an incredible ride down the backside, often at speeds upwards of 55 mph. The summits do challenge you, but they don't torment you. The wind, however, will. It will haunt you, relentlessly taunt you, and then occasionally be your best friend. It is an invisible force. When you are on those lonely prairie roads with a 30 mph wind at your face, it is nearly impossible to make much above four or five mph no matter how hard you grind, and if you stop pedaling the wind will push you backwards. Having the wind at your side is like having somebody running along beside you, pushing on you, trying to knock you off your bike. The wind will drive you mad. Of course, when it's at your back, the wind can push you along at an incredible pace. With a good tailwind you can sit upright, cross your arms, and with minimal effort make a steady 18-20 mph. Still, knowing the wind to be a fickle thing, we never wished for wind, from any direction.

{ MAYOR DON GERARDOT }

MONROEVILLE, IN
POPULATION: 1,236

....

"The biggest thing in my job is pursuing grant money.

It takes a person who cares about the community

they're representing and doesn't get rattled easily."

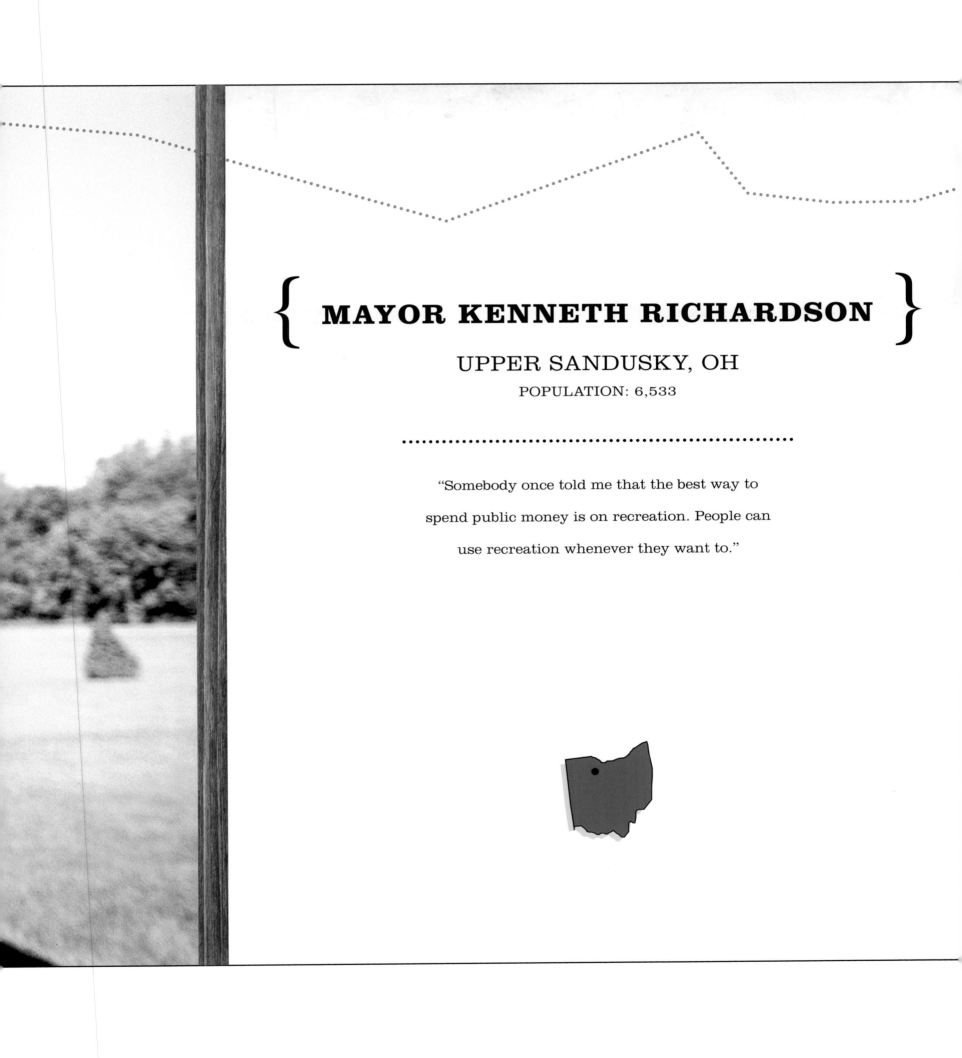

{ MAYOR KENNETH RICHARDSON }

UPPER SANDUSKY, OH

POPULATION: 6,533

· ·

"Somebody once told me that the best way to

spend public money is on recreation. People can

use recreation whenever they want to."

{ **MAYOR RITA MIDDLETON** }

CRESTLINE, OH
POPULATION: 5,088

....

Mayor Middleton is proud to be the first female

to represent her community and is working with

the citizens to address their needs.

{ MAYOR RICHARD WATKINS }

CANTON, OH
POPULATION: 80,806

....

"Government should do things for people

that people cannot do for themselves. It should

never do what people can do for themselves.

To me, that's bad business and bad government."

re generation.

Summer

{ **MAYOR JAMES SILEO** }

UNIONTOWN, PA
POPULATION: 12,422

"My objective has been to clean up the city, to get

law enforcement out there and bring the city back.

Bringing business downtown has been tough,

but I love this city, I was born and raised here."

{ **MAYOR LEE FIEDLER** }

CUMBERLAND, MD

POPULATION: 21,518

· ·

"The town took a big hit when the tire company moved out.

As a long time resident and former CEO of that company,

I felt it my duty to try to help out the town by serving as Mayor."

{ BACKSIDE }

....

It is important to ride as a team. It can be very dispiriting to look up and see your partner disappearing into the horizon. Over the course of the first few days, we found that we hit a good pace with Tim riding out front. So, for the better part of two months, I got to see a whole lot of Tim's backside. I could almost put together another book with all of the pictures I have - "Tim's Backside Across America". It is an unpleasantry with which you have to learn to deal. Next time I am riding out front.

....

{ MAYOR ANTHONY WILLIAMS }

WASHINGTON, D.C.

POPULATION: 572,059

....

"I think Mayors have a duty
to their community and their country.
Citizens need to look beyond themselves
and their own self satisfaction.
With freedom comes responsibility."

{ MICKEY IBARRA }

THE WHITE HOUSE

POPULATION: 281,421,906

....

"As the Director of Intergovernmental Affairs, I serve as
the White House link to city and small town government."

{ **MAYOR DEAN JOHNSON** }

ANNAPOLIS, MD
POPULATION: 35,838

. . . .

"It happens to be 'bike to work week,' so I thought I would

join you boys for the last few miles into Annapolis."

·············· **ACKNOWLEDGMENTS** ···············

My sincere thanks to each Mayor for taking time out of their busy schedules to participate in this project. To the citizens of each town through which we passed, I thank you for your generosity and hospitality.

My deepest gratitude to my long time friend, Tim Hovey, who joined me on this adventure enthusiastically and cooperatively. The goals I had set were lofty. Tim embraced them as his own from the outset and we worked as a team to see them fulfilled. A trip of such scale and duration is guaranteed to test the durability of a relationship. I am proud to say we remain best friends. His patience, persistence, and general good nature played no small part in the success of this project.

At the outset of this project, before we even began riding, a handful of very generous folks offered their support in order to help make the trip possible. Special thanks to: The Alexander Family, The Armstrong Family, Eric Barr, Vosteal Bateman, The Callenberger Family, Eliot & Debra Crowley, Mr. & Mrs. Charles Foster Sr., Mr. & Mrs. Charles Foster Jr., Bonnie & Richard Huckaby, Tom & Mary Lou Brown-Jewell, Mayor Harriet Miller, Art & Tassie Morris, A. Newth Morris III, Jane B. Morris, Kathryn Ann Morris, Michael Newth Morris, A. Newth Morris IV, Andrea Morris Shea, The Snoddy Family, and Russ & Barbara Widstrand.

Several organizations also supported the project in varying capacities. I would especially like to thank the faculty, staff and administration of the Brooks Institute of Photography, and Matt McAllister and crew, of Clear Channel Santa Barbara's 99.9 KTYD Early Show. I would also like to thank the following organizations for the products and services they provided: Aweto Custom Printing, Calumet Photographic, Color Services, Hazard's Cycle Sport, Jandd Mountaineering, Mountain Hardwear, Patagonia, Spin Dog Cycles, and Specialized.

It has been my experience that it is far easier to ride a bicycle 3,600 miles across the United States than it is to publish a book. I struggled on my own for a number of years, and at no small expense, to see the book you are holding finished. Here, I would like to thank Rich Wysockey who pushed me to see this book not merely finished, but complete. Without his encouragement I would not have continued the pursuit. That would truly have been tragic, for I would never have come into contact with Jeff Parker and Geoff Akins of AkinsParker Creative. They, with their team, elevated this project to the highest level, tied the story together, and presented it beautifully. I would also like to thank the Ueberroth Family for their support. Many thanks also to Debra Crowley and Jane (Sue) Morris. I owe each of them a box of red pens.

I would like to thank my father for all of his support. I was truly honored to have him join Tim and me for the grueling "downhill" 180-mile C&O canal leg. Given that his favorite remark concerning that bit of riding is "After that dude, my two cheeks didn't talk to each other for weeks", I am not sure he would do it again, but I know that he could. I would also like to thank my mother. She is and always has been supportive and loving. Without her incredible support in the "fourth quarter" this book may never have been.

For all of the contributions made by these many great people, organizations, and anyone I have unwittingly overlooked, I am truly grateful. However, it must be said that over the long course of this project, from concept to completion, there has been only one person who has never wavered in their support. She has never ceased in her generosity, never entertained notions of doubt or failure, and most importantly never stopped loving me. To my wife: This book is, as we are, something that grew out of youthful aspirations into something meaningful that will last a lifetime.